The Right To Depart

New and Selected Poems

Louis Faber

Plain View Press
P. O. 42255
Austin, TX 78704

plainviewpress.net
sb@plainviewpress.net
1-512-441-2452

Copyright Louis Faber 2008. All rights reserved.
ISBN: 978-0-911051-30-8
Library of Congress Number: 2008938999

Cover art by April Laragy Stein.

Dedication

To Elaine, who is truly the light of my life. She is my muse, my joy, my partner, and my editor. She illumines the dark moments, and brightens even the sunniest day. She can take the simplest events and make them seem new and magical. Her love of words reminds me why I write, and her writing is an inspiration to me and all who read it.

And to Mystie, who knows purr-fectly well why.

Acknowledgements

Grateful acknowledgements are due to the editors of the following publications where some of these poems first appeared.
"Into the Brush" in *Amethyst Review (Canada)*; "Another Ghetto" in *Ariga*; "An Off Year," "The Cemetery, After the Battle" in *Arnazella*; "Hanging By a Thread" in *Cairn*; "Parsings" in *Aura Literary Arts Review*; "Uncle" in *Cold Mountain Review*; "Akeda," "Deep In the Void" in *European Judaism*; "Enslaved" in *Footworks: The Paterson Literary Review*; "Reflections" in *Greens Magazine (Canada)*; "Map Store" and "Speaking in Tongues" in *HazMat Review*; "Drinking Tea in Kabul" in *Hearsay: Poetry By Lawyers*; "Backstreet Temple" in *Japanophile*; "Curfew" in *Kimera*; "Missing Persons" in *Leapings*; "Akeda," "Albert and I," "An Off Year," "Another Ghetto," "Auschwitz II," "Backstreet Temple," "Baghdad Villanelle," "Censors," "Deep in the Void," "Dust and Ashes," "Elegy for a Poet," "Hanging By a Thread," "Interactive," "Israel's Justification for the Bomb," "Kannon," "Map Store," "Missing Persons," "Ode to the Gods," "On the Tenth Plague," "Piano Lessons," "Small Reflection," "Speaking in Tongues," "Taos, Evening," " The Cemetery, After the Battle," "Unto Tarshish," "What Did You Do," "What, She Asks, Does a Feather Sound Like?" and "Yiddish" in *Legal Studies Forum*; "Dream On My God," "Dust and Ashes," and "Elegy for a Poet" in *Living Poets (U.K.)*; "Chicago" in *Main Channel Voices*; "To a Poet, To the West" in *Midnight Mind*; "On the Tenth Plague," and "Yiddish" in *Midstream*; "Israel's Justification for the Bomb" in *Pearl*; "Censors" in *PKA Advocate*; "Questioning God" in *Poetica Magazine: Reflections on Jewish Thought*; "Small Reflection" in *Rattle*; "Harlan" in *The South Carolina Review*; "Baghdad Villanelle" in *Thema*; "The Rabbi" in *Vent*; "Cosmology" in *Troubador: Best of Rhyme*; "What Did You Do" in *Vigil (U.K.)*; "Trickster," and "Unequinox" in *Yesterday's Laundry: Prose Poems*.

"Indigone" is reprinted by permission of River Light Press, from *The Sky Above Us, The Air We Breathe*, (c) 2007.

"Taos, Evening" is reprinted by permission of River Light Press, from *Illuminations: Fire, Light and Heat* (c) 2008.

"Kafka" is reprinted by permission of Birch Brook Press, from *Kafka Kaleidoscope*, (c) 1999.

Contents

The Right To Depart — 9

The Sea	11
The Mesa	12
Sensing	13
Unequinox	14
String Quartet	15
Shoulder City	16
Winter Dawn	18
Bottle	19
Manual Labor	20
Breath	22
Censors	23
English Class	24
No Difference	25
Unto Tarshish	26
Midstream	28
Taos, Evening	29
Dream On, My God	30
Vineyard	31
Morning After	32
User Interface	34
Remembering Another Father	35
Morning Sky	36
Small Reflection	37
Interactive	38
Elegy For a Poet	39
Harlan	40
Contemplating Suicide	42
Knowing	43
Indigone	44
Background Noise	45
Opening	46
Chicago	47
Into the Brush	48
Into the Tide	49
Aubade	50
Italo	51
To a Poet, To the West	52
Triangulation	53

Piano Lessons	54
Winter Stroll	56
Rolling Stone	57
Signs Of Age	58
An Ending	59
Jazz Night	60
Albert and I	61
October	62
This Poem	63
Waitress	64

Deep Into the Void   65

Map Store	67
Drinking Tea In Kabul	68
What Did You Do	70
What Do You Say	72
Asked and Answered	73
Lights	74
Kafka	76
On the Tenth Plague	77
The Cemetery, After the Battle	78
Everything In Its Place	80
Ode To the Gods	81
Hanging By a Thread	82
A Lesson To Teach	84
Enslaved	86
Trickster	88
Old Men Sit	89
Into the Fog	90
Waiting Your Turn	92
Following Orders	93
Missing Persons	94
Who Was That Masked Man	96
Auschwitz II	98
Deep In the Void	100
Arrival	101
To the Mothers: Rehoboth and Gaza	102
Gone	104
A Song	106
Gabriel, At Home In Ohio	108
Early Morning	109
Questioning God	110

Rushing In	112
Erato Sucks the Big One	113
Because	114
The Gifts	115
Parallelogram	116
Hear Our Prayer	117
Israel's Justification For the Bomb	118
Baghdad Villanelle	119
Curfew	120
Chaperone	121
Dust and Ashes	122
Yin, Meet Yang	123

Buddha and Hillel Dine Together — 125

Double Espresso	127
Quantum	128
Another Ghetto	129
Reflections	130
Raga Badva	131
An Off Year	132
Uncle	133
Holy Moses	134
Humanity	136
Boundary	137
Yiddish	138
Parsings	139
What, She Asks, Does a Feather Sound Like?	140
Adam's Rib	141
The Rabbi	142
Musings	143
Genesis	144
The Nature Of Magnetism	145
Papal Edict	146
Akeda	147
Harmony	148
A Different Sky	149
Cosmology	150
Return From Nineveh	151
Kannon	152
The First Jew On Mars	153
Peripheral Vision	154
Sanctuary	155

Speaking In Tongues	156
Breeze	158
42	159
Backstreet Temple	160
OT	161
Buddha and Hillel Dine Together	162
About the Author	163

The Right To Depart

The Sea

Sitting on the shore,
I asked the sea
to tell me of life.

The sea said the sky
      was a hungry suitor
      always trying to devour her.
The sea said doves
      no longer lived
      atop the mountains.
The sea said men
      embrace war
      because they fear love.
The sea said the moon
      could float indefinitely, but a man
      would drown of impatience.
The sea said women
      seek out peace
      because they are peace.
The sea said stars
      sing lullabies that we
      are too old to hear.
The sea said people
      pray to their God
      and make God their scapegoat.
The sea said life
      is a circle
      that man can not draw.
The sea said that nothing
      is permanent, there are
      no answers, that we all have
      the right to depart.

The Mesa

The coyotes come down from the Sandia Hills onto the mesa. They are not spirits. They are not totems. They are not tricksters. They are hungry: for a jackrabbit, for a bird, for a small dog wandering too far from a half-lit earthship. They smell the sage, its faint odor carried on the night. Taos, its weak glow on the horizon, is a spirit. It is a chindi to be avoided. It is the home of the skinwalkers. Out here only fools and shaman walk. There is no moon this night. The coyotes have no need for a moon. The stars are not mythic creatures cast into the heavens. They are points of light, collectively painting the black dome. They bathe the sage and desert earth in light. A cry in the distance: a brother has been fed. Coyotes don't mourn the jackrabbit. His purpose has been fulfilled. An elk bellows from across the asphalt ribbon or across the canyon carved by the river. They know the river as more than a rope of water flowing beneath the bridge; the bridge on which men stand and marvel. The coyotes have tasted the river. A jackrabbit cries. A brother or sister howls. There is a chorus. There is silence. Later, as the sun first appears behind the mountains, the coyotes retreat into the hills.

On this mesa, in its surrounding hills, are the bones of many jackrabbits and many men. There are the bones of the coyotes as well, all mingling in the dry, stony soil.

Sensing

"Turn on the light
so I can hear you,"
she says, and I reach
for the switch across the room.
"Please whisper," I respond
"and I may be able to see
my way to the window."
I draw up the shade
and in the dim glow
of the night's light
I feel the braying
of a coyote in the Sandia hills
and taste the chill
of autumn that wraps
the house in its soft
blue-black velvet grip.

Unequinox

A robin is slowly building her nest. She sits on one of the higher branches of our still winter-naked maple. She anxiously tucks small twigs, weaving the impenetrable. Each time I walk beneath she sits up and chides me. She is an expert in propriety.

My lover and I walk down a rutted path, grasses worn down by our predecessors. We walk for half a day, half an hour. Time does not matter. We stop to rest. We are encircled by towering pines. Several, I know, want to collapse onto a soft bed of needles. All want to pry open the sky. Neither she nor I remember why we are here. Shards of passing clouds ignore us, offer no answers. Our fingers interlace. Did I do this? Did she? My skin is wrinkled, dry bark. I have been in this forest once before, I think — perhaps that was a dream. I do not say this. For her this is new. She is awed by redwoods, something so large, something so fragile, how does it lick at heaven without retribution? My lover smiles: "I have been places like this, but never here." The sun retreats slowly, parting beams shimmer through slivered breaches in the canopy. The chill of onrushing evening draws us back along the path. We step in each other's measured footprints. We startle a robin from a margining bush. It flies angrily into a forced solitude. Dusk cedes the reluctant sun.

I walk past the barren maple: the robin stares down at me. Passing beneath her, the sun breasted bird whispers: "We prize our peace and remember those who would deny it to us." It is night.

String Quartet

The violinists' laughter and tears
are flung from her flying bow,
drip from his elbow —
wash over the stilled audience —
we can taste the sea
as we threaten to capsize.

The viola is the older brother
now steadying, now caught
in the wave, riding
its dizzying course,
dragging us in its wake.

The cello is a torso, the cellist
a surgeon, her hands
plucking small miracles
from stretched gut,
shouting for, then at,
the still stunned gods.

Somewhere, Brahms
must be smiling.

Shoulder City

The morning silence,
or such as there is of it
in the heart of the city,
is broken by the screech
of locking breaks, a horn,
and the almost pregnant pause
hanging in the heat, for the sound
of grinding, bending metal —
a sound that this morning
remains filed away, saved
for another day, a different
intersection, an alternate time.
In the fifteenth floor lobby
of the Holiday Inn a group
of Japanese pose en masse
for photos, one dropping in
to the scrum, another
sliding out, taking up camera.
The athletes, bags slung over
chiseled shoulders, queue up
at the elevators, chittering
among themselves like
squirrels around a walnut tree
after a strong wind brings
a torrent of nuts to ground.
Some press against one another,
fingers intertwine, glances pass
with impish smiles, young lovers
off for a day in the city, off
to the volleyball courts, the pool,
the start and finish lines painted
on the too-hot asphalt.
Only the old couple stares with scorn,
expressing silent derision as
one man kisses another
for luck, for love, as two women
stroke each other's hair —

day four of the Gay Games
is about to begin. The streets
swallow them all up,
and the morning silence,
or such as there is of it
in the heart of this city,
is long forgotten.

Winter Dawn

A sudden
December morning,
and a chill precedes
the arrival of the sun.
I watch for clouds
over the hill,
that will swallow
both the Sun
and winter.
The cardinal
pecks at a sour cherry.

Bottle

The bottle sat forever
on the naked oak sill,
gold in the fading day.
I don't remember how
it got there, how long it sat.
We ignored the silent cry
of the grapes seeking release,
the carefully corked Burgundy
sun faded into a sterile night
as the bottle waited,
sweetness ebbing,
growing acetic in steps
too small to measure.
One day I noticed
it was gone, all
that remained was
a water stain,
a broken ring
that marked our passage.

Manual Labor

      (Instructions for Mourning a Marriage)

It didn't come with an instruction manual,
no simple, poorly translated diagrams
telling me to "be inserting Tab A
into the Slot B," none to be found.
I was young and didn't worry,
despite entreaties to get help first
before beginning the intricate task of assembly.
I laid out all of the parts carefully
until it looked about right, and made
my own checklist, noting each part in detail,
smug when I found that all were present
including some without discernable purpose.
I cobbled together a small toolkit,
things that appeared like they might work,
set about the laborious task of building it.
It went together fairly easily, logical connections
made, wires twisted and wrapped in small bits
of duct tape, until it took shape and function.
I reached out gingerly for the starter switch,
depressed it with great trepidation.
It began to hum, its gears crawled to life,
meshing almost seamlessly, with only
the occasional groan, shake and click
from some dark corner of the machine.

For some time it worked reasonably well,
with occasional starts and stops,
nothing a little oil didn't correct.
Every now and then I would find the odd part
left in its wake; for a while
I would put them in a drawer in my desk.
They grew too numerous, and since it
kept sputtering along, I slowly discarded them.

Now, I can't tell when it happened, since
I long ago stopped checking it,
but one recent morning I turned to it

and it sat, refusing to move, static.
I pushed and prodded it. It sat.
I changed its battery. It shuddered and sat.
I took it to the repair shop and they stared
until one of them laughed and said,
"There is absolutely nothing we can do, we have
no idea how it worked this long, all we can say
is give it a proper burial, and next time
do yourself a favor and read the fuckin' manual."

Breath

In the night
there are no demons,
just the sound
of your breathing,
soft, as your touch
on my back,
your foot against
my calf.

Censors

They stole his words,
carefully sidling up to him
when he was distracted,
plucking one left
hanging from a pocket;
or in his room at night
sliding one from the dresser.
He never saw them
and never suspected.
They toyed with him
for a while, taking
only verbs, leaving him
transfixed and cursing his pen,
for reasons none could fathom.
One morning, lost
in the first sun of spring,
they took nouns,
and his world became
more vague and indefinite.
Now and again, in moments
of boldness, they would take
a phrase or, when
he was particularly vigilant,
merely a letter that would
not often be missed.
His world grew darker,
quieter, his notebooks sat
patiently awaiting his return,
but he had less and less to say
and covered the window
of his study with an old tarp.
He cried in increasing silence
until, caged within his skull, he
was left to stare at the vacant
walls seeing nothing.

English Class

He had planned
the exercise for weeks,
certain this one
would help them
break through the walls
that imprisoned
the metaphors within them.
It was simple — that
was its beauty — too many
attempts had become
bogged down in
the fear that words
could do the greatest harm.
"The exercise is simple,"
he said, and they
put pens to paper.
Toward the end
of class, "Would one of you
be kind enough
to read to the class
your description
of a young woman's lips?"
One boy meekly rose
and through half clenched
teeth said, "Her lips
were precisely shaped
to barely cover her teeth."

No Difference

I took the road
less traveled by,
and still haven't found
my way home.

"I need some space,"
she said.

"I'll give you all
of Montana," he said
" if you want —
all but Bozeman —
that I'm keeping
for myself."

Unto Tarshish

In this place
there is a fatted,
sacrificial silence.
It is the large
Jewish Cemetery
nestling the road
where Maryland
and the District are loosely
stitched together.
It is a small plot
of yellow-gold dirt
outskirting Lisbon.

This ground is sacred,
not for the blessing
of one who
has taken the tallit,
the sanctity of this
ground leaches
from the simple pine
boxes that return
with the bodies
to the soil.

The stones, mostly simple,
with neatly incised
Hebrew inscriptions
are all blank
to me, worn
smooth by memory
denied.
 I place my ear
carefully to each, wanting
to hear a voice,
a fractured whisper
that will resonate
in the hollow spaces.

I pass by those
with shared names,
for if he or she is here
each must share
the isolation
they willed me.
   I look
at the faces
of passing mourners —
no one resembles
the morning mirror.

I grow tired
of the search, sit
in the paltry shade
of the Ricinus plant,
knowing we both will
be gone by sundown.

Midstream

A young man sits
on a large flat rock
jutting out into a river.
He slowly tells the river
the story of his life,
places he has been,
people seen and known.
Each passing drop of water
hears a small bit
of his story, none
hears the whole.
Some time later I sit
on the flat rock
and stare into the roiling water.
I listen for the river's story
but each drop of water
tells small bits of its life,
or maybe it is
the lives of others
who stood along its banks
and let their lives
trickle into its flow.
A fish swims slowly by,
its silvered scales
flashing gold
in the late afternoon sun.
It pauses near the rock,
purses its mouth
but swims off downstream.
We both understand
it is only the ocean
that hears us fully.

Taos, Evening

On the mesa
between El Prado
and Tres Piedras,
after the sun
is swallowed
by the mountains,
to the east a fire burns.
Countless stars
stare down
on the shivering sage.
The scorpion lunges
for the distant hill.
The fire grows
behind the mountain,
the white-orange disk
rises slowly.
The smallest stars
flee Luna's furious light.
The jackrabbit
stands frozen
in the road
until her baleful eye
falls on him,
and he dives
into the sage.
In the dead hours,
once Luna has
sought her refuge,
the clouds are
no longer shrouds.
The wind
fancydances
in the canyons.

Dream On, My God

Good night Sisyphus,
try and get some sleep.
It's been a long day
and you already know
the rock will await you
when you arise in the morning.
I suppose by now
you've come to realize
there is no percentage
in pissing off the Gods.
Think of this as a personal
reeducation center
where right thinking
is the lesson of this
and every other day.
Did you really think
they would let you stand
in the middle of the square
openly mocking
all of their edicts?
Sleep, old fellow,
we have all the time
in the world — it is
one of the benefits
of immortality.

Vineyard

These plump, yellow-green grapes
clustering under brittle looking leaves
may never grace our table,
never grow legs
in a fine crystal wine glass,
never be described
by nose and palate,
finishing long or crisp
or even bright and balanced.
No one scores them
on a 20 or 100 scale,
they have never tasted oak.
Standing amid these vines
under a late August sun,
the cluster of grapes
growing heavy in my hand
is simply potential
to be realized, or not,
but in this moment
also a promise
of the perfect Chardonnay.

Morning After

Two bottles, the Pinot Noir upright
in the slant light of early morning,
its tubular sides carefully aligned
awaiting the wine, long ago poured.
Its yellow-orange label is a yin-yang
half in the unfiltered sunlight
through the partly open window,
half hiding in the shadow of the room.
The other is more bulbous, Chardonnay,
greenglass from the first annealing.
It has rolled across the table,
its gently curved sides begging
to be rocked, even uprighted.
Each bottle is so different, one
darkness, one light,
horizontal, vertical
and in the corner of the glass table top
two corks nestling together,
breathing deeply, whispering
of the night's events.
The echo of the late night conversation
has faded into once white
plastered walls, but I strain
to hear it. Was it a tale of great love
found and as quickly lost, the darkness
of betrayal, the clear light
of revenge; or a collective
search for a path to enlightenment
as lids grew heavy under
the vine's stare; perhaps a debate
that danced the sharp edge of civility
over the relative merits of dactyl
or spondee; a broad condemnation
of the G8; screenwriters who grow

so enamored of a line, it survives
long after their narrative arc
has perished painfully in the mouth
of the best actor the budget could buy.

No, the corks whisper, none
of those, but a workshop in real
time of how to jury-rig
a set of calipers when you're halfway
from Taos to Santa Fe
and the wheels come off.

User Interface

U: Cope.
I: How?
U: Relax.
I: Can't.
U: Why not?
I: No time.
U: Make time.
I: Takes too long.
U: Better idea?
I: None!
U: Tried?
I: Can't.
U: Why not?
I: No time.
U: What then?
I: No idea.
U: Can't help.
I: Why not?
U: Tried.
I: How?
U: Suggested.
I: That's all?
U: Cope.
I: How?
U: Relax.
I: Can't.
U: Why not?
I: No time.
The System has suffered a critical failure
and will shut down –
all unsaved work will be lost.

Remembering Another Father

It was scrawled on the back of a grocery receipt, barely legible. Charles H. Boustead Tunnel, fryingpan river. The river is lower case, its capitals dangling by serifs in one of the tunnel grates that constricts the water's flow.

Outside, the full moon is ensnared in the gnarled, barren branches of the white birch. She struggles vainly to break free, but the maple wraps its limbs around her. It is only when she retreats into the earth, covers herself over, that the trees cede their grasp.

When Luna curls against you, is she chilled from the night sky, or does she reflect the warmth of the distant star? Does she press against the shredded satin, wrap herself in the fringe of your kittel? And when she tires of you, does she leave by the rotting, split pine boards through which you, bit by bit, return to the soil?

I stand outside, shivering under a full January moon. Fading impressions of you are shunted into the tunnel of my memory. I never know where or when they will emerge, what they have gathered, what has been lost along the way. I hope for their return, regardless of form. The Boustead Tunnel carries about 54,000 acre feet of water annually from the river to the Turquoise Reservoir.

Morning Sky

Overhead a red tailed hawk
cuts a perfect circle
into the sky.

Standing below, looking
up, I imagine myself
with great feathered wings
able to break free
of the binding earth,
to rise up and cut
a perfect circle in the sky.

Above, the hawk
stares carefully down at me
and imagines a field mouse.

Small Reflection

It is that moment when the moon
is a glaring crescent,
slowly engulfed,
when the few clouds give out
their fading glow.
In the jaundiced light
of the sodium arc street lamp
it nestles the curb — at first a small bird —
when touched, a twisted piece of root.

I want to walk into the weed-strewn,
aging cemetery, stand in the shadow
of the expressway, peel
the uncut grass from around her head-
stone.   I remember
her arthritic hands clutching mine,
in her dark, morgueish apartment, smelling
of vinyl   camphor   borsht.
I last saw her in a hospital bed
where they catalog and store
those awaiting death, stared
at the well-tubed skeleton
barely indenting starched white sheets.
She smiled wanly and whispershouted
my name ~ I held my ground
unable to cross the river of years,
unwilling to touch
her outstretched hand. She had
no face then, no face now, only
an even fainter smell of age
of camphor   of lilac   of must.

Next to the polished headstone
lies a small, twisted root.
I wish it were a bird, I could place gently
on the lowest branch of the old maple
that oversees her slow departure.

Interactive

He slides into the bed after she is long asleep. It is a well rehearsed routine, and she senses his presence from deep within her dreams. He leans into his wife, traces his finger tip down from her temple, along the line of her jaw, into the hollow of her neck. In his dream she has grown younger, more beautiful, as he has bent under the weight of time. In this dream, she dances around him, her feet never touching the floor into which he slowly sinks. As the birds begin their morning symphony, she wakes and slips silently from the bed, her gaze lingering on his slowly graying beard. She kisses him lightly on his cheek, and in his fading dream he reaches the cragged peak of the mountain. He smells the scent of pine, then the faint lavender of her pillow, as she steps into the shower and he eases into morning.

Elegy For a Poet

(for Allen Ginsburg)

You died quietly in your bed,
friends gathered around,
the cars and buses of the city
clattering out a Kaddish
to a God you had long ago
dismissed as irrelevant.
We would have expected
you to howl, to decry
the unfairness of it all.
You merely said
it is time, and slipped away.
Who gave you the right
to depart without leaving us
one last remonstration
against the insanity
that surrounds us, one last
censure of the fools
who we have so blindly chosen
to lead this generation
into a hell of our creation.
You had your peace,
but what of us?
To what can we
look forward
in your absence,
save the words we know
so well, can recite by heart,
one that no longer beats
in your breast.

Harlan

You came, Harlan, to Rochester
somewhere in an endless winter,
"Ellison in Tundraland" you said.
We all chuckled approvingly.

You said a short prayer
climbing into the rusting Opel,
sliding on the edge
of oblivion, and
the approaching snowplow.

You stood, hoarse, smelling
of Borkum Riff and English Leather,
tweed jacket over polo shirt
and thinning jeans.
You told us of the insanity
of television, a medium
pandering to idiots.
We nodded, hoping
you would finish before
the Star Trek rerun.

We sat in *Pat and Sandy's*
as you consumed two orders
of fries, and a dwindling
bowl of ketchup. Later
we sat in the *Rat*, staring
at the empty bottles
of Boone's Farm until
you took pity and ordered
two pitchers. You were
our patron saint.

Solzynitsyn was exiled
to a cabin in Vermont,
staring as the leaves greened
then fell under winter.
You served your banishment
in the land of lost souls,
miles from any reality.

Contemplating Suicide

She stands on the bridge
and stares down
into the slowly flowing river.
She wonders what it
might feel like
to climb the railing
and, pushing off, gain flight.
The river would welcome her,
enfold her, carry her
to its heart. She
will not leap this day
just as she did not
the day before, but
she often has this conversation
with the ever-changing water.
She reaches
into her pocket, pulls
out a penny,
throws it into the river.
She does not make
a wish, nor does she
feel wishes are foolish.
Today she merely wants
to see the polished coin
glistening in the sun, it's
copper golden reflection,
as it tumbles in
its downward arc.
This is sufficient for her
on this day as on most days.
She walks off the bridge.

Knowing

She wants to know
if I could be an animal,
which would I choose.
Part of me wants to answer panther —
sleek, black, catlike, eyes
glowing in the night;
never coyote — crawling out
of the hills in search of rabbits
darting through the sage,
never the trickster.
I am an animal, I remind her,
we all are, just a bit smarter than most.
She laughs and says
I really wanted to be a god
since I had the image part down.
I say I'd thought of that,
but as a human
I get two days off a week
and God, according to Genesis,
got only one, and
he probably spent it
watching football in New Orleans.
She says she would rather be
a dragon or a fox since Shinto gods
have far less work to do
and generally sit around
being simply venerated.
I close my book, listen
to the rain pelting windows,
watch the bolt
flash crazily across
the face of the clouds,
listen for the peel of thunder.

Indigone

I have always wanted
to walk into a store
and buy a rainbow.
I have seen rainbows in stores
but never the one I want,
one marked down because
it is missing a color,
perhaps indigo. How
would we know
if indigo were truly missing?

Last week the clouds, the sun
and a post-rain mist conspired
to raise a rainbow in the eastern sky.
I saw it clearly, though it did not
seem anchored to a distant horizon
as so many rainbows are.
I made an offer,
but when the clouds huddled
with the sun to consider it,
the rainbow slipped away.
I asked the clouds and sun
if they would look for it.
No, they said, rainbows
pretty much come
and go as they please.

Background Noise

They took him far out onto the mesa
where the faintest lights faded
into the oblivion that space provides.

He was of the city, its people his tribe,
its buildings, that reached seemingly
for the gods, his reservation. They sat

in silence among the sage.
They asked city man if now
he heard the stars, but he heard

only the wind, and then the bray
of coyotes, which rose into
a chorus, and were again silent.

Listen carefully, they said, surely
you can hear them as you see them
set above, across the tapestry of sky.

He heard only coyote, the pierced
cry of a too slow rabbit, not the
stars, or the gods they formed, names

he memorized years earlier.
Focus your ears they said,
for coyote answers the song

of the stars, of the spirits they
are, taken from us but ever watchful.
City man smiled wanly as he climbed

back into the car to begin the journey
to his concrete reservation, and as
they bid him a final farewell,
they mourned his deafness.

Opening

In a bit less
than an hour
a new exhibit
will open,
empty space will
be occupied
with moving
bodies of artist
and viewer,
universes will form,
a thousand children
will be born,
an old man in
a distant city
will slip away,
a contented look
pressed into
his face,
world leaders
will ask why
and have
no answers.
All of that
is not now,
but in a bit
less than
an hour.

Chicago

This muscular city
is defined by
great blocks of stone,
hewn granite,
limestone, transfixed
along the aortal river,
its asphalt arteries,
churning by day,
now quiet.

In the hollow hours,
when the city
lumbers into sleep,
the clack
of my heels echoes
off polished marble,
is gathered by the dome
that caps the lobby,
reflected back
metronomically skewed.

Half a country distant
my lover is
curled in sleep —
the cat, unmoving
nestles her feet.
I hear her breath
in the breeze
that slips beneath
the brass framed entry,
see her smile flicker
off the slowly revolving door.
The languid look
of the desk clerk
distracted from his book
urges me
to the elevators.

Into the Brush

I have carefully peeled
back the skin of a hundred snakes,
left their twisted forms
curled around mesquite
as so many skirts. Canada geese
follow carefully worn paths
across an October sky,
undeterred by storm clouds
giving chase from the west.
A wolf wanders down
from the tree line to the edge
of the highway. She tastes
the approach of winter,
bitter on her tongue. Her coat
grows thick, watching
for a buck to be thrown
to the gravel shoulder
by a passing truck.
In my closet I have
a pair of boots, nothing more
than simple cowhide.

Into the Tide

The woman at the next table
stares at her fork
with eyes that appear
bottomless pools of sorrow.
She picks at the noodles,
raises and lowers
the glass of wine
without sipping.
She is lost within herself —
even the waiter
approaches with trepidation
for fear of falling in
and drowning
in her sadness.
Her eyes
are pools of cabernet
spilled from glasses
cast aside
by retreating lovers,
the blood of a mother
who died in her birth,
tears of a father
hopelessly alone.
She sees him returning
to the table
and a smile of faint hope
crosses her lips,
lingers a moment
and fades
into her eyes.
She watches him
finish his wine
and with a questioning nod
of his head, drink hers,
as she sinks back
deep within herself.

Aubade

The sun peers through
the skylight, sneaks
catlike up the comforter.
He strokes her cheek,
they are drawn together,
lips touch,
toes twine,
hips press,
fingers trace,
the mattress is a world
of infinite gravity.
Downstairs
the cat
paces angrily,
the coffeemaker
thirsts for beans.

Italo

This is a poem
written inside the back cover of
If on a Winter's Night a Traveler.
If I were Calvino, this would
be in Italian with that hint,
however faint, of Havana.
At 53, if I were Calvino,
I could look in the front
of this volume and realize
I had some 9 years left.
Would I shift from poetry
to a forced prose, try
to publish books at a pace
of one a year, or stay
with verse, measuring lines
as surely as I might
measure the days past
and those remaining.
Better still, let me circle
each noun in this book
or even this poem,
replace the noun
with that seven later
in the giant unabridged dictionary
that causes a sag in
the oak bookshelf, for that
is what we would do,
isn't it, Italo?

To a Poet, To the West

Richard Wilbur lives in Massachusetts
and in Key West, Florida according
to his dust jackets. If you set sail westward
from San Diego you may find your dream
of China, the endless wall which draws
the stares and wonder more foreboding,
more forbidden even, than the city
which you visit to sate yourself of lights,
sirens, the blood heat of steam grates.
It is far easier than digging, far less
dirty, and the walls of the sea rise
more slowly. Once it was a risky journey
the danger of the edge looming over the horizon,
but then digging was no option, pushing deeper
with your crude shovel, knees bloody,
until, at last, you broke through
with dreams of the dragon as you fell
into the limitless void. Now you sail
with dreams of the Pacific sky, although
water has no need of names. The poet
has grandchildren now, and it is to them
to dream of the China that was.

Triangulation

He says that, foremost,
Mao Zedong was a poet
and knew that all poetry
must at some level
be political, must
incite the reader to rebel
against complacency.
I say that Zhao Zhenkai
wrote as Bei Dao,
the ultimate act
of rebellion, sacrificing
his very identity.
He says that I
am anchored by
the weight of realism,
and I say that he
needs reeducation.
She says that neither
of us will ever write
the just opened bloom
of spring's first rose.

Piano Lessons

Mrs. Schwarting was my piano teacher. When I was twelve, my parents gave me a choice of lessons: piano or dance. I had two left feet. I chose piano. It did not move. My mother smiled at my choice. She knew what my decision would be before she asked. My mother was like that.

Mrs. Schwarting was my piano teacher. Each Wednesday at 4 P.M. mother dropped me off in the driveway of the cottage-like house, hidden in the cul-de-sac. I waited on the ivy covered portico until the prior student left. I never knocked on Mrs. Schwarting's door. No one ever knocked on Mrs. Schwarting's door. No one ever came in with me. Piano was something I learned alone.

Mrs. Schwarting was my piano teacher. Her hair was the gray of a Buffalo winter, a sky promising snow. Her hair was the pale blue of a sky bleached by the August sun. Her hair, she said, was once blonde, like autumn wheat. Each Wednesday I took off my coat and hung it on the single hook by the door. One hook, she said, one student. One year I played a duet with Larry Feldman. Each Wednesday Larry's coat or mine would lie on the floor. One hook, one coat.

Mrs. Schwarting was my piano teacher. Her first name was Mrs. That's what my mother wrote on the check I always put in the little basket on the top of the piano. Once, my mother forgot her checkbook. She gave me cash. When I put it in the basket, Mrs. Schwarting clucked her disapproval, "no bills, only checks. Please to vait on porch until your mother arrives." The door closed behind me: "no bills, only checks."

Mrs. Schwarting was my piano teacher. She was five foot one. She would stand behind me, "keep spine straight, zat is how you must play," her head hovering on my shoulder like a pet bird. She smelled of lavender, her breath of slivovitz. She was German. Her house was German. Her English was German. Her piano must have been German. It loved Bach, Beethoven and Brahms, tolerated Mozart but despised Satie. "It is the fingers," she said, "the piano cares not." The piano cared.

Mrs. Schwarting was my piano teacher. Czerny was her mentor, she said. "You vill play each piece at least fife times each day. Each day, fife times. You vill write down each day how many times you play each piece." Each day I sat at the piano. I played each piece five times. One day I lost

count, and played one piece a sixth time. My fingers felt guilty. I played it badly. When the sun was out, the only tempo was presto. I always played fortissimo. Mother listened. Mother counted.

Mrs. Schwarting was my piano teacher. Each May she would hire a hall for a recital. We would sit in "just so order, not to move, not to speak, just to sit. You vill never look to your hands. Zay are at zee end of your arms, I am certain. You vill play slowly. If you play fastly, you vill play again." Mrs. Schwarting was German. Her house was German. Her piano was German. Her fingers, which always tapped my shoulder to set the tempo were German. I told my mother she was a Nazi. My mother laughed, "she's just German." I thought, maybe, she was Eichmann's secret lover. I thought maybe she was Schumann's love child. I never liked Schumann.

My sister took lessons from Mrs. Schwarting. She thought Mrs. Schwarting's piano was German. My sister could reach a full octave easily, I had a span of a seventh. In my last recital I played Für Elise. I played it badly.

Mrs. Schwarting was my piano teacher. In the lobby of the Osaka Westin Hotel there is a piano. At three in the morning, fresh from a trans-Pacific flight, I wander the lobby. The desk clerk smiles. I sit at the piano. My back is straight. I play the opening ten measures of Für Elise. I still cannot reach an octave. I play it badly.

Winter Stroll

We walk together
getting even closer.
We talk to each other,
our hands touch.

The park path is covered
by ankle deep snow.
It crunches under our boots,
if it cries in pain
we aren't able to hear it.
Our footprints remind us
where we have been
if only we look back
to see them in the snow.

We talk of our own pains:
of loves that have left us,
those we left
out of fear or self-preservation.
We recount tears we shed
for people who exist only
in memories that shift
like the sands of the desert,
threatening to be carried off
on the next strong wind.
When spring comes
we will inhale the blossoms
of lilac and dogwood,
of loves and lovers
that were perfect in their moment.

We walk together
as snow begins to fall
filling in our footsteps,
slowly erasing our passage.

Rolling Stone

Early one May afternoon
Sisyphus said fuck it all
and headed off to Florida
in his beat up VW Microbus.
The giant rock rolled downhill
and came to rest in the creek,
seriously pissing off
trout that kept banging
their heads tying to leap it.
Outside Ocala his water pump
gave out, its ghost laughing
as he stood in the downpour
pushing on the van
as torrents washed his feet,
he mired in the mud.
Night fell as the State Trooper
wrote out a citation
for an expired registration
and drove back to barracks
leaving the old king by the roadside
dreaming of Fort Lauderdale
and wet T-shirt contests.

Signs Of Age

1.
I wrote a note
to remind me
to remind you
of that thing
you didn't want
to forget, but
I can't remember
where I put it.
Have you seen it?

2.
I am rapidly
approaching the point
when counting black hairs
on my head is easier
than counting years.

3.
This year I finally
remembered your
birthday — now
if I could only think
of your name.

4.
In the mall last week
I walked excitedly
into "The Body Shoppe"
only to find
they don't sell
replacement parts.

An Ending

We fled the sound of lightning,
took refuge deep
within purple, grew slowly
blind
        we felt our way,
tracing walls —
one room, two, in blackness —
there is no counting, just
moving in a slow waltz
following the measured
rhythm of deafness,
two dancers, one dance.
We collapsed in corners,
time and space converging
into a prison, we dared
not move for motion is
risk anted and the pot
far too hot to carry.

Jazz Night

The cat only wants to go outside. It is night, her favorite time, and she stalks the uncoiled garden hose, a fierce snake that falls to her attack. The man and the woman are dead tired, drowned in the fifth night of the fourth annual jazz festival. His shirt is bathed in the half dry dampness of sweat. She sags as though ligaments have shut down. He sinks into the sofa, uncertain if he can rise. The cat returns to the side door triumphant, the mighty green striped python left motionless on the walkway. Later, as he waits for the woman to finish her shower, the man sheds the shirt, but the saxophone and trumpet cling to him, even under the fine spray of the shower he can still smell the brush stirring the snare and cymbal. It is only later, deep in sleep, that the pillow absorbs the last chord of the guitar.

Albert and I

Time folds in on itself,
the arrow bends, grows recursive –
we lapse slowly backward
slipping into a protean state.

Our universe is neatly resected,
the inner working laid open,
showing craftsmanship
far beyond our meager
comprehension – we cling
to the surface, fear
sliding into its depth,
spiral freely in infinite
progression, slowing, approaching,
never reaching the source.

We wash up on a beach, are pulled
from the earth, dangle from
the neck of the sun.

October

There is an infinite space
inside an atom, a massive void
into which universes tumble,
where stars and planets are born.
Outside, maple leaves
burning flame and crimson,
spiral to the lawn which
waits to receive them.
Autumn is the season
when the earth prepares to die
and it is left to us
to ready the gravesite.
The white squirrel stands
on the fence rail, defying
me to find my camera,
his latest nut husks
staining the concrete
of the walk. And yet
we cling to the fleeting sun
as it traverses horizons,
for winter brings nothing
and asks even less.

This Poem

will not marvel at the dawn
stare at the ebb and flow of the sea
see ghosts in the clouds over Dachau

will sit on the page staring back
remember the torn wallpaper
cry out, always unanswered

will not trace your spine, lingering on each vertebra
make childish sexual come ons
wipe a tear from your cheek

will curl next to me in a hotel bed
whisper to me when sleep flees my grasp
pervade my dreams.

Waitress

She says sometimes an angel
will appear, and you won't know it.
Driving US 1 out of Narragansett
the map says you are close to the sea.
You cannot smell the salt,
there is no scent of cod or clam;
there is only faith.
The waitress in the Newport Café
wears the uniform, plaid
shirt and khaki slacks.
You don't recognize angels, sometimes.
I said she was Russian,
my wife said she thought the girl
was French, the girl smiled.
I said she had the smile
of a *matryoshka* doll.
The girl said her name was Lidia, she
was Russian. Most men thought
she was Russian, most women
thought she was French.
I wondered if there was another smile
inside, and one inside that.
She didn't heal my sore back
or shorten the seven hour drive.
A day later I remember her smile.
Sometimes angels simply tell you
you don't need more than you have.

Deep Into the Void

Map Store

The bride walks down the aisle
trailing a veil of tears
rolling in the dust
of too many centuries,
encrusting the virgin.

Albert Einstein
purchases a map of Taos.

Bookkeeper hunches
over ledger sheets
tallying night winds across
the frozen pond, a lone log
wedged in the ice.

Douglas MacArthur
purchases a map of Hue.

Monitors blare news
from other worlds, flickering
across half empty cups of
coffee, cigarette butts
and muscatel dreams.

Rosencrantz and Guildenstern
purchase a map of Sarajevo.

Drinking Tea In Kabul*

Rockets flash briefly
across the chilled sky,
plumes of smoke,
ash, are carried off
by impending winter.

Over the lintel of the entry
to the Hotel InterContinental
Chicago, carved deeply
into the polished marble –
Es Salamu Aleikum –
staring implacably
through ponderous,
brass framed doors
onto the Miracle Mile.
Countless guests
pass below it
unseeing.

My son and I
sit across a small table
spilling bits of tapas
onto the cloth,
laughing lightly
at a young boy
bathed in a puree
of tomato, his shirt
dotted in goat cheese.
My son explains
the inflation of the universe,
gravitational waves
cast off
by coalescing binary
neutron stars.

His words pull me
deeper
into my seat.
We speak somberly
of the jet engine

parked haphazardly
in the Queens gas station
unwilling to mention
265 lives
salted across
the small community.

We embrace
by his door, our few
measured hours now spent.
He turns to call
his girlfriend,
I turn up my collar
against the November night.

The Red Line train
clatters slowly back
into a sleeping city.
In my room
I brew a cup of Darjeeling.

* "We will drink tea in Kabul tomorrow morning, if God wills it."
    Basir Khan, Northern Alliance Commander,
      quoted in the *Chicago Tribune*, 13 November 2001

What Did You Do

When they asked him
what he did during the war,
he said "I just stood guard."
When they asked him where,
he said "A station, just
a station, like most others,
I just stood guard."
When they asked him
did you see the trains
carrying bodies crammed
into cattle cars,
he said "I saw many trains,
it was just a station, but mostly
I looked at the sky, wishing
for the sun, mostly it was gray
and there was smoke
from the chimneys."
When they asked him
why did you wear
the lightening bolts,
he said "I was a ski instructor
but I broke my leg
so I stood at the station,
just a station like most others."
When they asked him
did he know of the ovens,
he said "They made bread
which we ate each night
when there were no potatoes."
When they asked him
about the Jews,
he said "I knew no Jews;
there were none in the town
where I stood guard
at a station, just
a station like most others."

When they asked him
what he did after the war,
he said "I prayed, just
prayed for my sins,
sins like those
of so many others."

What Do You Say

What do you say
to those who turn their backs
on those broken in battle,
or broken at the sight of battle,
who were left to clean up the collateral damage,
or were collateral damage,
who were pierced by IED's,
or shaped charges,
had inadequate armor
or no armor at all,
who were left in moldy rooms,
were dropped on the street,
who don't want to go back again, and still again,
who see clearly with their eyes closed,
cannot find shelter in a maelstrom of thoughts,
did what was asked
and wish they hadn't,
asked for leaders and found only followers,
asked why and were told "just because,"
who never came back,
who were left here.

Asked and Answered

You may ask again,
but the answer will not change.
Your truncheons may bruise me;
my brittle bones may shatter,
but the answer will remain the same.

You may take me from my village,
line me up at the edge
of the freshly dug pit,
gun me down with woman and child.
The sun will rise on the city,
the answer will hide in the alleys.

You may chase me to the border,
may hack me limb from limb
with your machetes, burn my hut,
deny our kinship. They
will pronounce judgment on you,
you will recall the answer.

You may place me in your camp,
you may reeducate me without end.
Your tanks may crush me
under their relentless tread.
You can direct me to forget
but the answer remains unchanged.

You may ask again
but the answer remains the same.
It is man's nature to seek peace.

Lights

For eight days each December
they call out to me as the flame
of the candles flickers out.
"Remember me," they say in unison.
"Remember me," in the voice of a child,
an old woman, in Yiddish,
in Polish, German, Czech, Latt.
I want to remember but I cannot see
a face reduced to ash, blended
into the earth of a farm field outside Treblinka.
The winter wheat remembers.
I want to remember, but I cannot stroke
the head of a young man whose bones
mingle with his brother's, countless others
sharing a mass grave, his skull
and thoughts painting the trunks
of a nearby stand of trees.
I want to remember, but cannot hear
the sweet tenor of the cantor
whose tongue was torn from his mouth
for refusing to speak of the tunnels
beneath his once beloved Warsaw.
I want to remember the lavender scent
of the young woman, fresh from the showers
but there is only the stench
of wasted flesh and Zyklon,
of bodies crammed into a converted boxcar.
I want to remember the taste
of a warm challah on Shabbat eve
that she lovingly shaped
into a braid and pulled from the oven,
by arms crudely removed
by the surgeon before she
was cast naked into the Polish winter.

I want to remember them all,
capture their names in a memorial
but they are only numbers
tattooed onto endless arms.
The candles die and their voices
fall silent for yet another year.

Kafka

June 13, 1896, Prague –
a warm day, an old stone schul,
you stood before the minyan
wearing the skullcap,
repeating ancient words
that lay on the skins, rehearsed,
sounding false on a tongue
swollen in anxiety.
Your tallit, white
woven with blue threads,
hung at your knees
fringe fingered, rolled
and unrolled, twisted
until touched to skin,
words inscribed, etched
into collective memory.
Seventeen years later
sitting with Buber
did words come back
and stick on your tongue?
Later still
when you studied
under Bentovim, did words
take form and shape?
Did they dredge
up a past kept suppressed,
walking in desert heat
knowing salvation was
down a hill, entry forbidden.
Lying in your bed
in Hoffman's Sanatorium,
the trees of Kierling blooming,
did you recite Kaddish
as endless night engulfed you.

On the Tenth Plague

Mark your doorpost with the blood
of the lamb, for this may be the night
when God's emissary arrives for the killing
of the first born. Will he be a night bird,
half raven/half vulture, or an aged man
concealing his weapon in shabby robes.

Mark your doorpost and check it
often, for if your neighbor wipes
the blood away, you will be visited
and no amount of pleading will
deter him from his task. There are
no interim plagues remaining to buy
you time, if he chooses to come tonight.

Put your ear against the window
and listen for him. Will he come
on cat's paws or the rale of lungs
slowly drowning? Will coins jangle
in his pocket, to pay your fare
to the ferryman?

But if you do not believe,
perhaps he will forget to come.

The Cemetery, After the Battle

They come to her in the dark.
The voices whisper, she hears them.
They sound like the children
that ran across an open field
chasing a ball, a bird,
a mortar shell whose fall
outpaced them, left them all
scattered, shattered, marked
by simple wooden crosses
later taken for heat.

She strains to answer them,
words thick on her tongue,
clogging her mouth
like a gas soaked rag
stuck in the thin neck
of a bottle. Lit, they explode
in her mind, shrapnel
tearing at her eyes
red, only red, the sky
seems aflame yet the sun
has long since set
behind the smoke of the fires.

They hover around her
gently touching her cheek
like a demented butterfly
seeking nectar long dry.
She caresses the thick scar,
but there is no feeling,
only numbness of too many bodies
strewn on tables, across chairs
broken to feed the flames
which flit away into a snowy night.

She can see their masks
hiding sneering lips.
She curses them, faceless,
her eyes pressed shut
by their tiny fingers, kneading
soft dough, pulling it
taut, letting it snap back,
released by the ghost child who
runs laughing up the hill
chasing a dragonfly
into the dawn.

Everything In Its Place

He captured stray beams of light
in a small amber bottle,
which he tucked into a dark corner
of a shelf in his basement.
He canned a small bit of the sky,
sealed it carefully, placed it
in his pantry, for posterity.
He stored his collection of dawns
in an old cedar chest in the attic.
He had a bookshelf of genomes,
arranged alphabetically,
next to Mason jars filled
with ashes of victims
of each genocide
of the last five centuries.
It was the Greek amphora
perched on the mantle
that he most prized,
waiting for the day
when he could look
within it
and bid good morning
to his soul.

Ode To the Gods

You, who walked here
through the ages,
watched a million
suns swallowed
by untiring waves,
what is it you expect?
There is nothing here for you.
The spirits of the old ones
have long since fled
our sharpened blades,
retreated with stars
into the hills.
Animals will come
to you no more
for we serve them up
as a sacrifice to our hunger.
You gods are a paltry lot.
We take your names —
you are no longer —
and we drag our God
from within the mountain
to shine as a morning sun.

Hanging By a Thread

In Riga, my grandfather
was a master tailor.
The great and the rich
would come to his shop,
some bringing bolts of fine cloth
and others trusting him,
knowing that wools and silks
were not beyond his reach.
Even after they marked
his home as that of a Jew,
the Captain, who rode
through the city with his men
throwing torches through windows,
would come to him
late in the night,
seeking a new dress uniform.
Eventually they took his needles,
threw his spools of thread
into the river. He could stand no more
and with the few kopecks that remained
he left for New York
where, he thought, even
a poor tailor could walk
on golden streets and create
garments the likes of which
a Tsar could only dream.
Each morning he would arise
and strap on scarred phylacteries
to recite the morning prayers.
He would go into the cold
in his threadbare coat,
to factories and couture houses,
only to return before noon
to a bowl of bread soup,
await the visit of one
of the men or women in his tenement

who would ask him to sew
a patch into a worn jacket
or fraying dress, all
for a few pennies
begrudgingly spared.
He was the new Moses, he said,
free of bondage,
milk and honey
would be his portion.
He wandered the desert
of this new land, free
of the bonds that
had enslaved him,
plucking bitter manna
from the sands.
"I am free," he would shout,
"to starve on the cliffs
overlooking the land
promised to me."

A Lesson To Teach

This is what
I would tell my sons:
"You came from
an ancient people,
a heritage of poets
and tailors, of thieves
and blasphemers,
of callous men
and slaughtered children.
I would give you these books,
written by God some have said,
although I am doubtful,
but driven by Erato without doubt."

This is what
I would tell my sons:
"I didn't go to war —
there were so many options
and I chose one where
my feet would touch
Texas mud and tarmac,
where the only bullets
were quickly fired
on the rifle range.
I wasn't one of the 56,000.
I didn't come home
in a body bag.
But I do stop at the Wall
each time I visit D.C.
and say farewell
to those who did."

This is what
I would tell my sons:
"You have never known
hunger for a scrap of bread
pulled from a dumpster,
you have never
spent a night on a steam grate
hiding under yesterday's
newspapers from
the rapidly falling snow.
You never stood
nervously in the waiting room
of a dingy clinic
waiting for a young,
uncaring doctor to announce
that antibiotics would likely
clear up the infection
but you should avoid
any form of sex
for a couple of weeks."

This is what
I would tell my sons:
"You come from
a heritage of poets."

Enslaved

We are six hours out of Tokyo
somewhere over the North Pacific.
My back is cramped, calf muscles
knotted, longing for sleep
that will not come, a movie
rolling out in sullen silence.
I wait for the night to pass, for light
to break in through the cracks
around the pulled shades,
some small reminder
that day and freedom await. But the sun
remains outside, knowing its place.
We wandered the desert for 40 years,
but there we had freedom of movement,
endless space in the parching sun.
Sitting on the plane, quietly begging
for a landing and the crush of bodies
moving through the airport, I long
to see her pull off the shirt and jeans,
to see her standing, stretching in pink
panties, to mix lust, love and sweat,
to hold her in the frantic moment of orgasm.
None of that is possible from seat 34-C,
United Flight 882 en route to Chicago.
We stood in the cattle cars, pressed
so tightly that movement occurred
only in waves, surprised that they
would treat laborers in such a fashion,
but dreading the alternative,
constant provision of your papers
to smug young men who knew so little
of the world, save for the gray wool
uniforms, twin lightning bolts
screwed into their lapels. Their cruelty
was not only expected but ordered.

When we saw the smoke rising from the ovens,
we knew, preferred to deny the truth,
as surely as the cordwood knows that it
is destined for the fire, soon to be ashes.
She is waking now, stepping from the shower
her skin lightly red from the back scrubber
and the towel rubbed across her thighs.
We stood on the deck of the old freighter,
many of us pressed against the rail,
saw the old seaport baking in the sun,
a land we were certain was promised us.
They turned us back, though several drowned
swimming for her shores, death preferable
to returning to a place of nothingness, a void.
Six hours out of Tokyo, teeming with people
like the lower East Side on Shabbat morning,
I want to see open spaces, find some sort
of freedom, find slavery barely
a bitter memory, saved for prayer.

Trickster

> "Coyote is always out there waiting, and Coyote is always hungry."
> Navajo Saying

Dusk cedes slowly into violet night. A crow flies across a near full moon. Coyote comes down from the foothill wearing a mask.

I met her in a letter Jewish Family Services wrote in response to my request: "We are barred by law from giving you identifying information concerning your birth parents." Buried within the third paragraph was this: "Sixteen months after your adoption, your new parents adopted a baby girl, Lisa." She was formless, this sister. My adoption was an accepted fact, predating memory. She was to be my sister, a baby growing into my reflection. She came and left in half a line of a letter, a quickly fading echo.

Sitting in the cramped office, the caseworker, hair backlit through the window, the gray-blue of a half clouded summer sky, rested wattled arms on a stack of files. "About your sister I know almost nothing. Your father died when she was four months. We had no choice but to take her back. We placed her immediately with a new family and lost touch."

I am a watcher of name tags. I search for Lisa's, estimating ages. I have no pictures. Mother burned them when they took Lisa away. I still recall the smell when she threw the baby blanket into the fireplace. I remember now how smoke choked the room. We fled the house. She never mentioned Lisa.

Coyote is two fiery gems across the mesa. Coyote wears the mask of a caseworker. Coyote comes down from the foothill and steals a small child. Coyote's bray is mocking.

Old Men Sit

Old men sit
on concrete benches
at the end of the park
and kvetch, about their checks,
about Morris who died last week.
Young men
turn uncomfortably in their graves.

Old men reflect
on their wars, peering
across trenches,
hiding from gas clouds,
inching forward, friends falling.
Young men
turn uncomfortably in their graves.

Children play
amid the shell craters
and dream of a war
where their sticks
can be traded for guns.
Young men
turn uncomfortably in their graves.

Young girls
place flowers on headstones.
Where once they watched
the games play out, they now
dream of their fallen heroes.
Young men
turn uncomfortably in their graves.

Into the Fog

"Dad, where were you,"
he asked over dinner,
"when John Lennon was shot?"
Or where, for that matter, was I
when Jim Lovell calmly said
"Houston, we have a problem."
When John Kennedy died,
I remember sitting on the floor
staring at the TV, feeling
the warmth radiating from
the pipes buried in the floor
as my brother crawled,
slowly around the room,
trying new words and falling
onto the dog, who merely scowled
and shifted his hind end.

I remember sitting on a hill
overlooking the televisions
gathered just below, as Neil Armstrong
gingerly stepped down,
two thousand Boy Scouts
staring in rapt attention. I
pulled my ponytail from beneath
the neckerchief and wondered
when the mescaline dream
would fade into sleep.

I have been here fifty-three
years, seen a billion suns
fade into the void,
a billion more congeal,
cast faint tendrils of heat
across an endless gulf.
I have seen torn bodies of children
litter a small village

in the central highlands of Vietnam
and streets of Sarajevo,
seen the bloated bellies and toothpick limbs
of children in the Mogadishu dust,
heard the first cries of my sons.
"I don't really recall
where I was when Lennon died,"
I told him between leaves of artichoke,
"but I remember thinking
what an utterly insane loss it was."

Waiting Your Turn

The man
in the next bed
died last night.
You were sure
it would be you.
You were ready.
He never unpacked;
thought his visit
would be short —
he'd be home
in a couple of days.
We never
pause to think
God revels
in irony.
Why else
was He so generous
with fire: Prometheus
had to steal it.
To us it was a gift
we shared freely
with Hiroshima
and Auschwitz.
Sleep, it
is not yet
your time
even if you
wish it to be.

Following Orders

Forget us they say,
make it as though
we never existed,
act as if we
defied our orders
and stopped the trains,
opened the gates,
let them slip
into the Polish winter.
Do not recall
how we whipped
the crowd into a frenzy,
stood idly by
as the mob shattered
the glowing windows
of the sanctuaries
and built pyres
for the prayer books.
There is no reason
to remember
how we patrolled
the walls and fences
of the ghetto,
how we shot
even children
who dared crawl out
in search
of a crust of bread.
Forget us they say,
as you would
any lost generation,
and let us rest
in this cold earth.

Missing Persons

I enter the station house
and walk up to the neck high desk.
I would like to report
a missing person.
I have been gone
more than twenty-four hours.
I can't give
a very good description.
My eyes see in the mirror
a still young man
sitting in a park
in Salt Lake City passing
the joint and jug of wine.
My ears hear a voice
deep and rich, reverberating
through the microphone
preaching subversion
to the youth of Rochester.
My fingers touch the cheeks
of a girl perched next to me
on the outcropping overlooking
the middle falls, down from the Inn,
the sun dancing
off her long brown hair.
My nose smells the sour odor
of JP-4 Jet Fuel,
the exhaust of the F-102,
the beer soaking the floor
of the base NCO Club
late in the evening.
I taste the salt
of the sweat in the hollow
of her neck as we lay,
in a moment of reflection
amid a day of passion,
the Bahamian sun
beating down outside our window.

Sergeant, if you find me
please call me immediately.
I am terribly concerned
at my absence. It is
so out of character.

Who Was That Masked Man

Standing before the mirror
in the bathroom this morning
I saw an aging man who
could no longer remember
the look of a full head of hair,
what he was almost three decades ago,
when all his senses were more intense.
Now he stares at the familiar face.

I was not there, I say to him,
when we rode into Wounded Knee
and carefully decimated the tribe
like God's avenging angel.

I was not there, I say to him,
on some back road in Mississippi
when we stood in the truck bed,
looped the rope around his
black neck, drove off just
enough, watched him swing,
his blackness blending into the night,
framed by the flames
that licked his gas soaked body.

I was not there, I say to him,
in the small flophouse
across the street from his room.
Nor did I take careful aim
when he stepped outside
to greet the small throng
that had gathered in the parking lot
for a chance to cheer the dreamer.

I was not there, I say to him,
marching in neat rank order
across the quadrangle, my weapon
aimed at spoiled sons and daughters
of failed parents. When they
refused to disburse
it wasn't I who raised
my M-16 to my shoulder
and felled four
on a cold Ohio morning.

I was not there, I say to him,
in My Lai. It wasn't me
who torched their hooches,
gathered them in the rice paddy
and emptied a clip
into men, women
and children.

I was not there, I say to him,
and he smiles back at me
saying "I know, but
where were you,
and what would you have done
had you been there?"

Auschwitz II

when you lined   us up
neatly in order   as per the selection
and led us   to the "shower"
we knew   we would never
have to wait   our feet freezing
for another count   we would be checked
off your roster   logged and counted.

when we heard   the first hiss
from the shower heads   we knew
we would be   finally cleansed
and we poured out   our lungs
onto the whitewashed   walls.

when the young boys   piled us
onto the cart   we lay
perfectly still   so as not
to shift   making their work
that much   harder.

when they dragged us   into the ovens
we licked   at the flames
as they   shrouded us
quickly consumed   a paltry meal
for the inferno   always demanding
more.

when our ashes   rose into
a crystal blue sky   we stared down
floating over   the starved fields
we settled   slowly into the soil
knowing we   would yield
a thousand   bitter harvests.

when you visit us   your tears
bathe us   and we
are cleansed   while they
rub themselves   raw
and crawl   into the freshly
dug pits   marked
by simple stones   worn
we devour them   and they
cry out   Why?

Deep In the Void

There is
a mote
in God's eye,
the ashes
of the 6 million.

Arrival

The lake arrives each morning, just before she opens her eyes. She tried to catch it, getting up earlier or later but it was already lapping the shore outside her window each time she first gazed at it. Once she tried to stay up all night, and it clung to the shore despite its desire to slip away, but she was certain it did when her eyes fell closed a little after 3 a.m. She got up at the usual time, and it slid in just ahead of her. All that day it seemed quieter, almost restive, as if, like her, it lacked the energy that sleep might have provided.

She remembered her grandmother saying that only once in her years along the lake did she ever catch it just coming in around the point. That was a magical day, never repeated, but it bound her grandmother to the lake in a way few could understand. She kept asking her grandma to tell the story again, but like that day, she'd told it only once and would just smile when asked to repeat it. She never told anyone else — she learned as a child of the scorn she would face if she did. She gave up Santa and the tooth fairy, but this was real. She could touch it or even take it home in cups or buckets. Though, she smiled, it always slipped away sooner or later.

She knew from the doctor's face the chemo hadn't worked. She could feel it failing even as he pumped it into her. It was okay, she wanted to tell him, but it wasn't — they both knew it. They tried, won some battles, lost others, but in the end they both knew who would win the war.

This morning the lake never arrived, never touched the shore, and the house was shrouded in silence.

To the Mothers: Rehoboth and Gaza

(In memory of Amichai and Darwish)

To each of you
who have never spoken,
who would lack the words,
which of you is Hecuba
or are you both?

Your Priam leaves
each morning for the drive
to his laboratory
where he will spend the day
scribbling on the board.

Your Priam leaves
each morning in the dark
for the drive into Israel
and the mop and broom
he pushes through the halls.

To you a Hector, you a Paris
and you a Cassandra,
each sitting at the feet
of the elders, each
learning the stories of a people.

You watched as your Abraham
fell in the flames
of the Kaytusha, as your Ibrahim
collapsed in the rain
of the soldier's Uzi.

You watched as Ari
was pulled from the plane
in the black bag,
home from the Golan,
the fresh earth waiting.

You watched as Ali
was returned to Allah
his broken body
hidden in the box,
the mob of settlers dispersed.

You saw another son
hectored by a boy
who spit on his body,
stepped on his groin,
kicked him in the head.

You watched as your home,
the place of your birth,
was reduced to rubble –
by the car bomb, by the
army bulldozer.

You were left
to prepare the grave
of the son of your son,
felled by the rubber bullet,
brought down by the stone.

To each of you
who have never spoken,
who lack the words,
I wash you
with my tears.

Gone

The salmon people
don't live here anymore —
you have moved them
up the river, then inland,
so they no longer need to wander.

The salmon
do not swim here anymore —
you have dammed rivers
to draw out power,
penned the mighty fish
where the river first licks the sea.

The eagle doesn't
fly here anymore —
the great pines
that grew for generations
below his aeries are now
cut into neat supports
on which we hang our walls.

Our children
do not run here anymore —
they have moved
to cities, have gone
to wars, for fighting
is the only skill
which we taught them.

We have no rivers,
we have no salmon,
we have no sons, save those
who sleep under stones.
We look for the eagle,
its mighty spirit,
but he, too, has been claimed

to decorate their buildings.
We have only our spirits
to guide us and we know
that soon you will claim them too
and leave us, as you,
to repeat the sad story.

A Song

This is a song for the survivors —
for their ability to avoid danger
their cowardice and fear
their willingness to ignore
their facility to scorn heroes.

This is a song for the survivors —
for enduring degradation in silence
blending into the darkness
their imprisoned lusts
their emotional anesthesia.

This is a song for the survivors —
for their unnatural luck at the draw
their birth in one place not another
their skill of deception
their appetite for power.

This is a song for the survivors —
for their savagery
their cunning
their rage
their cruelty.

This is a song for the survivors —
for erasing the number
being someone else
sycophantic concession
trading on others.

This is a song for the survivors —
for praising their gods
offering their sacrifices
heeding their injunctions
their willingness to sacrifice.

There will not be a song for the survivors —
for their death will not be reflected
their death will not be recorded
their death will not be respected
their death will not be remembered.

Gabriel, At Home In Ohio

I saw an angel settle
slowly over Akron,
dancing in the smoke
rising from the stacks
of the ancient plant.
It flitted, darting in and out
of the gray haze, one moment
she, the next he, and as the sun
settled slowly, for an instant
no more than a cherub.
It was not, I think, a vision —
I had seen this before —
Ezekiel's fiery chariot
tearing through the sky
over the Mekong, only to disappear
into the heart of a small village —
again, careening madly
from the hills surrounding Sarajevo
until swallowed by the apartment block.
I saw an angel settle
slowly over Akron
dancing in the smoke.
I saw it clearly
from the window
of the Holiday Inn
until the night
swallowed it
leaving only bones.

Early Morning

Early this morning
as I drove through the mist
that clings to Portland in March
like a child's yellow slicker,
I thought of you, home,
asleep on our bed, my side
tidy, no faint indentation
of life. I thought of
the thousands who have died to date
in Iraq, who never again will leave
a faint indentation in any bed.
It is far easier thinking of you,
regretting the miles between us
at this moment, but knowing
that I will shortly bridge
those miles and tonight we
will both indent our bed.
Two thousand miles is
little more than an inconvenience,
while many of them are less
than a dozen miles outside of
countless towns; but the effect
of that short distance is infinite
and they now only indent the thawing
earth beneath the granite stones.

Questioning God

You shall love the Lord, your God
with all your heart, your soul, your might
even though you have nothing to eat
not a crumb, not a scrap,
and now are far to weak to stand.
And these words, which I command you
this day, shall be upon your heart.
You listen, you want to know
how will I face this?
Will you send me an angel
when the blade is about to fall
on Your sons and daughters,
or will it pierce their chests and Yours?
You shall teach them
diligently unto your children,
Will they hear you,
learn your lessons
with their faces pressed
into the rotting wood
of the boxcar, crushed
under the weight of the multitude?
And shall speak of them
when you sit in your house
and when you walk by the way,
when you lie down at night
and rise up by morning.
Can you frame the words
from a hollow organ
stripped of teeth,
each harvested
of its golden fillings,
a tongue taken
for an unspoken word.
You shall bind them as a sign
upon your hand and they shall be
forfrontlets before your eyes.

Perhaps the number tattooed
is mere Kabbalah, perhaps
it was no rope that held your wrists
to the chair back as they pressed
the battery cables to your groin
not caring if you
answered or not.
You shall write them on the doorposts
of your house and on your gates.
Perhaps next to the sign
that simply read
Arbeit Macht Frei.
That you shall remember
and do all My commandments
and be Holy unto your God.
And with six million voices
merged as one, you all say
Amen.

Rushing In

Step right up, don't hang back,
come and watch the fool perform for you.
You know me, bedecked in motley emotions
worn like so many colorful rags,
a suit of too many shades and hues,
all displayed for your entertainment.
See if you can find ten shades of anger
as I prance in front of you.
Count five flavors of tears
that start and stop like a passing storm.
Laugh at me as I pirouette, a dervish
who loved blindly long after
the love of my patron had died.
See me in my fool's cap, the bells
of rage and guilt dangling from its points.
If that isn't enough to bring out a laugh,
watch as I rip out my heart
and lay it at your feet, still beating
to the rhythm of the song
to which she long ago grew deaf.
Rain clichés on me as I stumble
across the stage. Though they ring hollow,
it is they I most crave, a redemption
that no monarch can offer.
Step right up, don't hang back,
come and watch the fool perform for you.
Do not pause to think
that you could as easily be here,
on stage, and I out there marveling
at you, wondering what you did
to deserve such a fate.

Erato Sucks the Big One

That one summer
I worked in the plant
I could hear them whisper
in the break room
with its ever empty
Coke machine.
They'd get real quiet
when I came in.
Some would nod hello
and quickly leave.
At first I thought
it was because I
was only there
for the summer.
But once, standing silently
outside the break room door,
I heard them talking
about the weirdo
who reads fag poems
when no one is looking,
how he is probably
some queer closet pinko.
I tucked my copy
of "Gasoline" in my back pocket
and wandered toward
my workstation, wondering
if Corso put
up with this bullshit.

Because

> "Poets are the unacknowledged legislators of the world."
> -Shelley

I write
        because words must be said
words must be said
        because they eat at my tongue
they eat at my tongue
        because they recall the flames of the ovens
they recall the flames of the ovens
        because they were forced to shower
they were forced to shower
        because they were Jews
they were Jews
        because they embraced Torah
they embraced Torah
        because they walked the desert
they walked the desert
        because they followed the manna
they followed the manna
        because it led to freedom
it led to freedom
        because I saw it in a dream
I saw it in a dream
        because a voice whispered it to me
a voice whispered it to me
        because I write

The Gifts

They brought him myrrh
on a flaming salver
and all he could do was say
"This is something I would expect
from a butcher or a carpenter,
the camera angles
would never work, so bring
me napalm or punji stakes."
They brought him ripe oranges
and the sweet meat of the pineapple,
its juice dripping from his chin,
and all he could do was tighten
his grip on the AK-47 and dream
of night on the edge of the jungle.
They brought him Rodin, Matisse,
Rembrandt van Rijn, and Blake,
but all he could see was
Bosch and Goya, and then
only by the light of fading candles.
They brought him the String Quartet
in A Major played on Stradivari's
and Guarneri's, but he
wanted the retort of the howitzer,
the crump of the mortar.
They brought him his child
wrapped in bandages,
and all he wanted was
the nursery, a newborn
suckling the breast,
as he stroked her head
and remembered the moment
of her creation.

Parallelogram

When I step up to the counter
place my bag on the scale
you stare at me in profile —

until your eyes
slip down to the small
Star of David
hanging around my neck.
I say shalom,
five thousand years
of history are piled
on your counter; you
stick a boarding pass
amid the clutter,
smile, say "Have
a good flight."

your eyes slip down
to the book of poems
Darwish, Adonis.
I say salaam
stroking my beard
absent mindedly.
You think
I am planning
to take the stack
of flight schedules,
you say only "Gate B-10,"
place a red dot
on my boarding pass,
smile at me
as I am escorted
to secondary inspection.

Hear Our Prayer

a voice cries out in prayer at sunrise
a voice cries out in prayer at sunset
a voice cries out in prayer outside the gates
        seeking entry into the holy city

the bride cries at the ancient wall at sunrise
the bride cries at the ancient wall at sunset
the bride cries outside the gates
        then enters into the holy city

the mullah cries out in prayer at sunrise
the mullah cries out in prayer at sunset
the mullah cries out in prayer outside the gates
        barred from entry into the holy city

Abraham cries out in prayer at sunrise
Abraham cries out in prayer at sunset
Abraham cries out in prayer as he
        unbinds his son from the altar

Ibrahim cries out in prayer at sunrise
Ibrahim cries out in prayer at sunset
Ibrahim cries out in prayer as he
        lowers his son into the grave

the soldier cries out in prayer at sunrise
the soldier cries out in prayer at sunset
the soldier cries out in prayer as he
        dodges a stone and fires into the crowd

Israel's Justification For the Bomb

Once it was fur hats,
men on horseback,
swords and torches
our villages casting a faint glow,
falling into dying embers,
here one whose skull
bears the mark of the hoof,
there an old one
who would go no farther.

Once it was a helmet,
tanks not horses,
flames contained in crematoria,
cities taken for the deserving,
we merely ashes
shoveled into a pit,
here a tooth, its gold
torn free and cataloged,
first the old ones
who could go no farther.

And so we have learned,
we in our kippot,
we in our planes,
and if you do not hear, we
will give you the fires of God,
you, your villages a faint shadow,
so much vapor, so much ash
carried on His holy breath as
we have learned well
and we have fused these words
in our minds: never again.

Baghdad Villanelle

We enter, the conquering heroes
drive quickly through the city's core.
We leave a crude division in our throes —

We expected flowers, not blows
of an angry mob. To be adored,
we enter the conquering heroes.

An old man sits in a small café, he knows
what will come of this, a festering sore
we leave, a crude division in our throes

that builds, wells up. We depose
a tyrant. You're a new tyrant they roar:
we enter the conquering heroes.

At home, on TV we watch the blows
rain down on the prisoners, huddled on the floor,
we leave a crude division in our throes.

We do not see bodies arrive, only rows
of new headstones. The President will say no more,
"we enter, the conquering heroes,"
we leave a crude division in our throes.

Curfew

We sat in the cramped kitchen
huddled around the stove,
the open oven door spreading
a faint warmth that barely
slid through the winter chill.
The bare bulb in the ceiling
strained and flickered,
fighting to hold, as the generators
shut down and darkness
enveloped our small world.
The sky was lit by the flares,
the odor of exploding shells
seeped through the towel-
sealed windows, covered
in tattered bed sheets
too thin to afford warmth.
Ibrahim had been gone two weeks,
sneaking out of the city
to join his brothers in Gorazde
or Tuzla, wherever it was
that they were struggling
to save what little was left.
We huddled under the small table
and dreamed of the taste
of fresh bread, or even pork.
In the morning Ahmed would run
along the cratered streets
in search of the convoy
and handouts which we
would raven as the sun set
over our war-torn hell.

Chaperone

There are three ducks on the pond
and none says anything
that is remotely profound.
Half a world away, a man
carefully parks a truck
at the edge of a crowded
Baghdad market and
walks quickly away.
Three ducks swim side by side
by side around the pond,
every now and again
plunging their heads into the water.
In Baghdad, safe
within the Green Zone,
the General says life
is slowly improving.
The truck by the market
does not explode. It
has run out of gasoline.
Stop and ask yourself
which of these three ducks
is the chaperone?

Dust and Ashes

Between Scylla and Charybdis
they cower amidst the ruins,
fearful to look skyward lest
they encourage the rains of hell.
Now and then they visit
the corpses, hastily buried,
grief drowned by the sound
of the laugh of the gunner
peering down from the hills.
It is always night for the soul
and lookout must be kept
for Charon, who rides
silently along the bloody rivers
that flow through her streets.
In great halls,
far removed from the horror,
self-professed wise men
exchange maps,
lines randomly drawn,
scythes slicing a people.
They trade in lives as chattel,
reap a bitter harvest,
pray there may only be
but seven lean years.
They offer a sop to Cerberus,
three villages straddling the river,
but the army of the hills
waits patiently for winter
when the odor of sanctity
no longer rises from the city
to assail their nostrils,
and Shadrach is
no more than a ghost.

Yin, Meet Yang

even as we pray for peace
> we continue to wage war

even as we continue to wage war
> we still much fear dying

even as we still much fear dying
> we live for the love of moments

even as we live for the love of moments
> we lie together as one

even as we lie together as one
> we bring forth a child

even as we bring forth a child
> we know he cannot bear arms

even as we know he cannot bear arms
> we persevere at profound worry

even as we persevere at profound worry
> we pray for peace

Buddha and Hillel Dine Together

Double Espresso

Buddha walks slowly into the coffee house
and orders a large mochachino.
He approaches the sofa in the corner
and folds himself neatly and precisely
into and among overstuffed cushions
to the delight of a five year old
pulling at his mother's sweater
as she struggles to finish her latte.
"The body," Buddha says
to no one in particular,
"is the finest form of origami
for even the great master Tsujimoto
has yet to duplicate it."
Constantly sipping at his always full cup,
he watches the comings and goings.
He picks up a dog-eared copy
of the Analectics from the table
and breaks into a wide grin,
"Good old Con," he mutters, "they never have
figured out how to translate you."
An old man stooped, half blind,
shuffles over and, in what
approximates a bow, says "Master
where can I find enlightenment?"
"My child," Buddha responds, unfolding
and refolding his legs and arms,
"why do you seek it — it won't bring you
much beyond what you have —
but if you truly wish to find it,
it lingers just behind you, so stop
looking, for surely it has found you.
Now let it catch you."
The Buddha unfolds herself slowly
pressing out the seams
of her plaid skirt and shuffles
quietly into the traffic along the avenue.
My cappuccino, I think, is now cold.

Quantum

The universe is both
enormously vast,
measurable only in metaphor —
and infinitesimally small,
an idea
that would fit
in the corner
of a grain of sand.
As you walk the beach,
grasp universes
between your toes
and kick them
into the cosmic tide.

Another Ghetto

She sits
in the bookstore café,
head covered
in a linen handkerchief
bobby pinned to her
mass of walnut curls.
She cradles a cup
of cooling coffee
and stares down
at the slim book
of Amichai, subservient
to the Hebrew letters
that seem to dance
across the page.
I sit at the next table
with my used
copy of Bialik, translated.
I glance at her
and say "I'll miss him."
with a nod to Amichai
and then "Where are you from?"
She smiles faintly,
self-conscious, "I am
from Atlanta."
"From what part?"
"Warsaw, inside
the walls and wire,
that place from which so few of us
ever managed to escape."

Reflections

An elk stands at the edge
of a placid mountain lake,
sees only the clouds
of an approaching winter.

A black bear leans over
the mirrored surface of the lake,
sees only the fish
that will soon be his repast.

The young man draped
in saffron robes looks
calmly into the water, sees
a pebble, the spirit of his ancestors.

I look carefully into the water
searching for an answer to a question
always lurking out of reach,
see only my ever thinning hair.

Raga Badva

Look behind the number, past
the curtain that shields
its magic from your eyes — it is
there the singularity of life sheds
its clothes, and what
you grasp so tightly
is no more than the idea
of dawn, the concept of death.
You must dig the grave
to that certain depth so that
should he ever arise, he will not
touch his head on the dew-
washed carpet that hides the sky.
Days in a week, denominator
of pi fractioned, I count
the Omer, seven times seven times
until the idea of a rest day
is as odd as the concept of night.
In alignment, numbers claim
kinship, six and six and six
devils stand aside and applaud
as sevens walk from the cliff
still waiting for the Word.
Your trinity is a unity —
infinity is divisible
only by zero and faith.

An Off Year

The was a winter, once,
where even in the north
the snow refused to fall,
ice rejected jamming the culverts,
and the sky stared down in amazement.
That was the year trees would not bud
and flowers fled deeper
into the sweetness of the earth,
grass sighed and lay indolent.
It was a year my coat of many colors
was taken, pieced out among brothers
until each had a color, none a coat.
I would sit at the right hand of kings
evisaging a day when dreams
might refuse to visit and
then, starved of images,
I could reinforce foundations
preparing for their visit.
I am strapped to the altar
and the knife is poised in the hand
of a man who would be a father,
both of us looking up for intervention.
There was a year, once,
when the ram broke free
of the thicket and picked his way
down the hill to his young.

Uncle

My uncle writes his journal
in cramped Yiddish: English
will not do, it lacks the words,
he says, to describe his world.

He describes the flavor
of the capon left to stew
on the stove, the sweet taste
of carrots and prunes.

He carefully notes the thumb
of the butcher sliding onto
the back of the scale, applying
just a quarter dollar of pressure.

He writes pages of
monologue, the slow twisting
of words stuck under his skin
like sharpened shoots of bamboo.

This language is sweet, he knows,
and when it is lacking, he
can reach to its roots
and graft a new word.

His journal sits on its shelf
gathering dust, its words
lost on my tongue, a tome
consigned to history.

Holy Moses

Consider, for a moment
      he said
         the absurdity of it all,
a guy with brains enough
           to shape universes,
   who can flick on stars
      with a thought
        faster than you or I
can throw a switch,
           who, worst case
     gives a lizard a kick
        in the ass
and ends up with man;
       that a guy with this kind of power
   is going to write his story
      down on a bunch of tablets,
or have an old coot wander
          the desert endlessly,
     pen and parchment in hand
       taking dictation,
   and then leave the scrolls
         scattered in caves;
it makes
     no freakin' sense.
If it was me,
     he said,
        standing on a hill
   watching some scrub pine
      slowly burn
no ashes, no embers,
    just burning;
        if I heard a voice
   giving me orders
      when I couldn't see anyone,
to go and slap
     some soldier upside the head
   or march into a river
      hoping to find stepping stones

followed by thousands of lemmings
                    lined up behind me:
                                        not this kid,
            me, I'd look for a screen
and some short professor
                        from somewhere in Kansas.
Do you buy
            for a minute,
                            he said,
        the he would wander
                    sucking sand from his teeth
and getting called
                    to haul his ass up a mountain
        for a crisis meeting,
                    and then to schlep
            tablets down the hill,
eating hardtack
                        and pretending to like it,
        telling his wife
                            he knew where he was,
                he wasn't lost,
so what
            if it was forty years.
                                        Miriam was really
        going to buy that,
                    and Aaron had to be
thrilled dragging the damn ark
                like a bloody albatross
                                then looking down into the valley;
            he's gonna say
                        okay, that's it,
go on without me,
                    I just got word
                                I gotta croak here,
        but keep a kind thought:
                            fat chance of that
                ever happening.

Humanity

Each day
I walk out
into the sea.
Each day
the sea engulfs me.
I cannot walk
on the water, nor
does the water part
before me.
Each day
I walk out
into the sea
and reconfirm
my humanity.

Boundary

What is on the other side
of this wall that is just
too tall to peer over?
No one seems to know,
though many have surmised
it is a completely different world,
looking little or nothing
like the one we inhabit.
Last week a young man
picked up a ginkgo leaf
and said, "Ahah, it is Japan
across that wall," but most
thought he was crazy.
Once, when the world was flat,
people knew if you sailed
too far you would fall off.
But the brave ones
always wondered what sort
of world existed on the other side —
was it desert or tropical jungle?
When it was night here,
was it day there or did the sun
simply sleep for ten hours.
This morning a young man
leaned a very tall ladder
against the wall and slowly,
carefully slipped over the top.
We shouted after him, asking
what it was like: did rainbows
look the same, was grass green,
but all we heard was his
retreating footfalls, and
his plaintive voice shouting:
"Eve, are you here?
I have the apple."

Yiddish

My grandmother lapsed
into Yiddish only on special occasions,
"Where other words won't fit,"
she said, "where there is
no English to describe
the indescribable, blessed
be He." We knew
that it was merely
a convenient way to keep
us out of the conversation,
while they clucked.
"Mah Johng is a game
that can only be played
in Yiddish," she said,
"to hell with thousands
of years of Chinese history."

She remembers the Golem;
she met him once
on Fourteenth Street
when she still had
the liquor store.
She thought it strange
that he wanted gin,
not Slivovitz,
but Golem can be strange
under the right circumstances,
and he did speak Yiddish.

Parsings

The old man sits
cross legged
on a grass mat.
A faint smile
glints across his lips.
He invites me to sit.
"Our meeting," he says,
"is *notable*."
I sit, legs
folded as best
I can, and ask
but he silences me.
"First tea." He
sets the cups down
on the hardpack
dirt floor. There
is *no table*.
He asks me
to listen
to passing birds,
the silence
of the sun.
I ask him
to sing a song
of the Way. He
is *not able*.

What, She Asks, Does a Feather Sound Like?

Echo of Galileo's ball
cast off the tower,
the cascade of butterfly wings
and universes collapsing,
the moment before there was time.

Adam's Rib

Adam's Rib was not,
she said, a barbeque joint
on Beale Street
in downtown Memphis
nor a beloved Spencer Tracy
movie in which sidelong
glances with Kate Hepburn
meant more than audiences realized.
It most certainly was not
proof of the claim that woman,
born of man, was meant to be
subservient for all time.
"No," she said, "Adam's Rib
was merely God's attempt
to get it right
the second time around."

The Rabbi

The old man peers at the yellowing book
then places it on the arm of his chair.
He gives the walker a sad, angry look
and still struggling, looks up in mocking prayer.
Clutching the book, he limps to the table
and sinks onto the chair, risking a fall
that could reshatter his hip. Unable
to hear, he shouts to his wife, down the hall;
she brings the hearing aid and his glasses.
His eyes glow as the ancient words bring fire
to his voice, arms dance as though his class is
full of young minds that are his to inspire.
He settles into the chair, bent by age
and curses his body, now more a cage.

Musings

The poet muses:
I wonder if a cat
purrs when no one
is in the room.
I suppose we could put in
a microphone and find out.

Schrödinger comments:
if there is no microphone
the cat is purring and
the cat is not purring,
and what is the half-
life of a poem?

Genesis

Cain slew Abel
in a moment of anger;
a crime of passion
would be his defense today.
We can only imagine
what Isaac might have done
to Ishmael, had Haggar
not been sent off by Abraham.
After all, he was a child
who saw the knife firsthand,
helped sacrifice
the thicketed ram.
Joseph tasted the pit
at his brothers' hands, was
mourned by his father
only to emerge and forgive.
It is little wonder
we Semites can't get along,
Jew and Jew, Israeli
and Palestinian, we've
been rehearsing this act
for millennia.

The Nature Of Magnetism

She cares deeply
that things fit seamlessly
together, that there be
no gap, no edge, no-
thing to interrupt the flow.
He loves the gaps,
the subtle shift in level
that can barely be felt
as a finger is dragged across
imperfections that
define uniqueness.
She wants the rose
fully petaled, will
dispose of it when
even a few have
settled onto the table.
He wants them to rest
there, to watch
as they dry, curl
and slowly bleed
their crimson
into the room's air.
Their two cats
think them both crazy,
but tolerate them
so long as their bowls
are filled twice each day
and the litter is changed weekly.

Papal Edict

She said "Now they've taken away limbo,"
sounding disconsolate,
"not that you proceed express
to the ferry dock, but
in a snap of a Papal finger, all
I was carefully taught
is suddenly wrong or irrelevant."
"It would be like Isaac,"
I say, "climbing Mount Moriah
with Abraham and finding a ram
tethered to a waiting altar."

My mother wants to know
how I can claim to be once-Jewish,
as though the moyel
also took my freedom of faith.
"We Jews have no hell," she
reminds me, "at least after death."
I try to tell her that
I still don't have a hell,
at least not as she conceives it.
"But I read," she says, "the *Tibetan
Book of the Dead*, and Buddhist
hell is very, very real."
I tell her my Buddhism is Chinese
through a fine Japanese filter,
that it is the next life
in which I will pay for this one.
She says "I wouldn't want
to come back again," and
on that point we find ourselves
at the edge of common ground.

Akeda

My father
never walked me
up a hill,
never asked
two servants
to wait below,
never bid me
be strong,
never asked me
to have faith
in the Lord,
never raised
the blade
only to see a ram
in a thicket.
My father
never did
any of these things,
and so I have
no special birthright
to pass to my sons,
for God
has moved on
to more
important matters.

Harmony

A young woman steps
from the shower and wraps
herself in a large blue towel.
"I don't want you to see me,"
she says, to the young man
standing in the door of the small
bathroom, "look away for now."
He reminds her they are married.
She says: "One thing has nothing
to do with the other, and
a husband must know his wife
by the contour of her chin,
the curve of her hip, the smell
of her slowly drying hair,
and the sound of her lips pursing."
She says: "When you can do
all of this with your eyes closed,
what need is there for sight,
and if you cannot, you
could have a thousand eyes
and still be blind."

A Different Sky

We lie on a hill
side by side, staring
at passing clouds,
discerning shapes, each
of us breaks into a smile,
each of us sees
a completely different sky.
After some time
I reach out, touch
her hand, our fingers
interlace, or perhaps
it is she who reaches
out to me, fingers intertwine.
It doesn't really matter
for once our hands
join, we each smile,
stare upward — we each
see a different sky.

Cosmology

Our purpose is to understand
and then explain
the inherent order of the Universe.
The logic of the array of stars
we see from our centrally located
observation deck, galaxies
so many fractals seeking
to hide their organization.
We have no ability to control,
lack the mechanisms
to make all but the most minute
adjustments, then only
to energize a stray electron
into a higher energy state.
We would like to foretell,
but we have no essential premise
on which to erect our framework,
just a cornerstone unwilling
to settle in place or time.
We can only recount
what we have learned,
cautious that we miss
only events of lesser importance
even if they are prehistory
long before they occur.
But this we remember:
before the beginning
was the beginning.

Return From Nineveh

Jonah, what color
is the sun at dawn?
> Black as the night preceding it.

Jonah, what is the odor
of Spring?
> That of rotting Ricinus.

Jonah, what shall we say
to a crying baby?
> The gates of Nineveh will be open.

Jonah, when God calls
how should we answer him?
> Call him sheol.

Jonah, we are soon to die,
how shall we face it?
> Crawl into the belly of the beast.

Kannon

The cats
at Senso-ji Temple
curl around
the incense burners
on a cold December morning
ignoring countless pigeons,
hopping impatiently,
awaiting flocks
of school children
in neat uniforms
and rainbow backpacks,
each with a slice
or two
of stale bread.

The First Jew On Mars

sifts red sands through gloved fingers,
kicks the small stone,
glares up at the heavens
the cold sun returning his stare,
and waits patiently
for the rain of manna,

looks vacantly across the landscape
and curses under his breath
at the absence of a good
lean pastrami and a half sour,
or even Chinese take out,

pauses to wonder why God
left so much unfinished,
an endless desert to be wandered
for countless lifetimes,
no further tablets forthcoming –
perhaps He was tired, needed rest –
each day is Sabbath,

struggles to remember
the holocaust,
the souls of a generation
whispering "Do not forget us,"

shouts the Shema
to the void, imagining
it falls on deaf ears.

Peripheral Vision

Open your eyes.
What do you see?
    The sky.
Close your eyes.
What do you see?
    Nothing.
Then open your eyes.
What do you see?
    The sky.
Close your eyes.
What do you see?
    Nothing.
Now open your eyes.
What do you see?
    The sky
      and a large hawk.
Close your eyes.
What do you see?
    Nothing.
Open your eyes.
What do you see?
    Nothing,
      it is night.
Close your eyes.
What do you see?
    Deep into the universe.

Sanctuary

The motion begins deep within you,
bleeds quickly outward
until it blankets the webs
between your fingers and toes, collects
behind your ears, as you hurtle
on parallel steel threads
connecting Tokyo and Osaka.
You cross the broad fields
of golden yellow beckoning
the impending harvest, the rice
swaying in the unfelt breeze.
In the furrow, neatly excised,
water burns with the gold
of the plants and the blaze orange
of the sun retreating
behind the mountain, tired
after a long day battling
winter's slow approach.
The stream is an intense blue,
out of place on this golden canvas,
a wound flowing to the horizon.
The cratered rim
of the great mountain casts
a winking glance at the rice.
It is a lookout for the moon.
In the fields are small huts,
some lit, in this hut, two men
bowing before a small altar.
I want to rise from my seat,
step from the bullet train,
wade through the rice
to join them, share a cup
of carefully brewed tea
and settle in their silence
under the watchful eye
of the guardian mountain.

Speaking In Tongues

She said
you should try
astral projection.

I said
I have tried
transcendental meditation
and even a bit of EST.

She said
that biofeedback
was better than
most of the drugs
she remembered using.

I said
that tequila
took far less practice
if you could stand
the inevitable hangover.

She said
she thought
that dying
was something
like giving birth

I said
that it was more
like an orgasm
that would last
an eternity.

She said
your coffin
would have
a weird projection.

I said
that hers
would have to be
surprisingly wide.

Breeze

The breeze slips
between ocean and mountain
bending the rice plants.
The earth is exhaling.

The breeze slides
between the leaves
which rustle angrily.
The tree is dancing.

The breeze skids
across the blades of grass
which try to stiffen.
The butterfly is carried off.

The breeze sighs
between my collar and neck
drying beads of sweat.
I bend my head in thanks.

The breeze skirts
between my pursed lips
caressing my teeth.
I sing a morning song.

42

    (for Doug Adams)

Before there was
a big bang
there was what.

Before there was
life
there was who.

Before there was
space
there was where.

Before there was
time
there was when.

Before there was

there was why.

Backstreet Temple

The afternoon sun
glares off the polished roof tiles.
The bells strung on the pagoda
of the small temple
tinkle in the wind.
There are so few
birds in Osaka.

OT

Standing in the garden,
in the downpour,
Eve turned to Adam and said
"Did you bring the umbrella?"
"What's an umbrella?" Adam asked.
"I'm eating the apple" Eve replied.

Buddha and Hillel Dine Together

The meeting occurred by chance,
two old men sitting in the same park
staring at the same empty chess board
as the waves of the Stygian Sea
lapped against the break wall,
the ferryman now at the helm
of a great cargo ship.
"So," said Hillel, "you come here often?"
Old, bent Buddha paused
"As far as I know, I have
always been here, or perhaps
I am not here now, never have been."
"I know the feeling" the ancient Rabbi said,
"I've been here so long, I too
have begun to doubt my very existence."
Buddha rubbed his great girth
and smiled placidly as a black bird
alighted on his shoulder.
The Rabbi stroked his beard,
stood on one foot,
only to have two blue jays
land, one on each arm.
"Would you care to join me,"
Hillel asked, "for a meal at Ming's,
or, if you prefer, we can do take out
from the Dragon Palace,
whatever suits your mood,
my treat this time."
The saffron robed old man
unfolded himself, and erect
and bowing, said
"It would honor me to dine with you
but, if you wouldn't mind,
I'd much prefer a bowl
of chicken soup with kreplach
and a pastrami on rye."

About the Author

Louis Faber is a corporate attorney and occasional adjunct faculty in English Literature at Monroe Community College. He and his wife, fellow poet Elaine Heveron, live in Rochester, New York. He began writing poetry in high school. His work has appeared widely in publications in the United States, Canada and the United Kingdom. In addition to graduate degrees in law and business, he also holds a Master of Fine Arts degree in Creative Writing from Goddard College.

www.ingramcontent.com/pod-product-compliance
Lightning Source LLC
Chambersburg PA
CBHW051438290426
44109CB00016B/1608